A Day in the Life: Polar Animals

Reindeer

Katie Marsico

 EAST RIDING
OF YORKSHIRE COUNCIL

Schools Library Service

PROJECT
February 2013

www.raintreepublishers.co.uk
Visit our website to find out
more information about
Raintree books.

To order:
☎ Phone 0845 6044371
🖹 Fax +44 (0) 1865 312263
🖳 Email myorders@raintreepublishers.co.uk

Customers from outside the UK please telephone +44 1865 312262

Raintree is an imprint of Capstone Global Library Limited,
a company incorporated in England and Wales having its
registered office at 7 Pilgrim Street, London, EC4V 6LB
– Registered company number: 6695582

Text © Capstone Global Library Limited 2012
First published in hardback in 2012
First published in paperback in 2013
The moral rights of the proprietor have been asserted.

Edited by Daniel Nunn, Rebecca Rissman, and Sian Smith
Designed by Joanna Hinton-Malivoire
Picture research by Hannah Taylor
Original illustrations © Capstone Global Library
Production by Victoria Fitzgerald
Originated by Capstone Global Library Ltd
Printed and bound in China by South China
Printing Company Ltd

ISBN 978 1 406 22883 0 (hardback)
15 14 13 12 11
10 9 8 7 6 5 4 3 2 1

ISBN 978 1 406 22890 8 (paperback)
16 15 14 13 12
10 9 8 7 6 5 4 3 2 1

**British Library Cataloguing in Publication
Data**
Marsico, Katie, 1980-
   Reindeer. -- (A day in the life. Polar animals)
   1. Reindeer--Juvenile literature.
   I. Title II. Series
   599.6'58-dc22

Acknowledgements
We would like to thank the following for permission to
reproduce photographs: Corbis pp. 7 (Frank Krahmer),
8, 23c (Christophe Boisvieux), 13 (Layne Kennedy); FLPA
pp. 5, 23b (Mark Newman), 10 (Minden Pictures/Colin
Monteath), 11, 23a (Minden Pictures/ Michio Hoshino), 14
(imagebroker/Horst Jegen), 17 (Minden Pictures/Michio
Hoshino), 20 (Minden Pictures/ Michio Hoshino); Photolibrary
pp. 4 (imagebroker/ Michael Krabs), 6 (age fotostock/ Mark
Hamblin), 15, 23f (Imagebroker RF), 16 (Oxford Scientific/
Daniel J. Cox), 19 (Imagebroker RF), 21, 23e (Imagebroker
RF), 22 (Oxford Scientific/ Mark Hamblin); Shutterstock pp.
9 (© Roman Krochuk), 12, 23d (© pzAxe), 18 (© Witold
Kaszkin).

Cover photograph of a reindeer (Rangifer tarandus) in snow
reproduced with permission of Alamy Images (© WILDLIFE
GmbH). Back cover photographs reproduced with permission
of Shutterstock: lichen (© pzAxe), antlers (© Witold Kaszkin).

The publisher would like to thank Michael Bright for his
assistance in the preparation of this book.

Contents

What is a reindeer?. 4
What do reindeer look like?. 6
Where do reindeer live? 8
What do reindeer do in the day? 10
What do reindeer eat? 12
What hunts reindeer? 14
Do reindeer live in groups? 16
What do reindeer do at night? 18
What are baby reindeer like?. 20
Reindeer body map. 22
Glossary. 23
Find out more 24
Index 24

Some words are shown in bold, **like this**.
You can find them in the glossary on page 23.

A reindeer is a large **mammal** that often lives in snowy areas.

All mammals have some hair on their bodies and feed their babies milk.

antlers

Reindeer have **antlers** on their heads.

Antlers are hard and look a bit like tree branches.

What do reindeer look like?

hooves

Reindeer have wide hooves which help them to walk on snow and dig for food.

Reindeer usually have fur that is a blend of grey and brown.

nose

Their thick hair keeps them warm during freezing weather.

Reindeer even have a special nose that warms the cold air they breathe.

Arctic

Reindeer live in a part of the world called the **Arctic**.

In the Arctic it is light all day and all night for part of the summer.

8

In the Arctic it is dark all day and all night for part of the winter.

The Arctic is one of the coldest and windiest places in the world!

W_ _t _ _r _i_ _ _ r _ _ in the day?

Reindeer are usually most **active** during the day.

They start their day by waking up and looking for food.

Reindeer travel long distances each year in search of food.

They often walk across frozen ground and swim through icy waters.

lichen

Reindeer eat **lichen** that grows beneath the snow.

There are lots of different types of lichen.

Reindeer use their hooves to uncover lichen.

They also eat whatever grasses and leaves they can find during warmer months.

golden eagle

Grey wolves, polar bears, and brown bears hunt reindeer.

Golden eagles sometimes attack young reindeer.

wolverine

Wolverines attack reindeer too.

People also hunt reindeer for their meat and **antlers**.

Do reindeer live in groups?

Reindeer live in groups called herds.

There can be dozens to hundreds of reindeer in a herd.

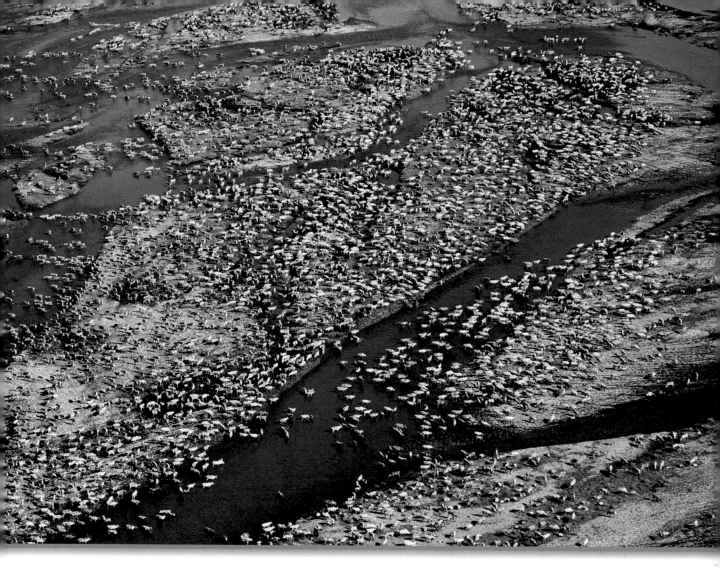

When reindeer travel long distances, small herds often join together to form large groups.

There are sometimes hundreds of thousands of animals in these herds!

What are reindeer doing at night?

Reindeer may spend part of the night looking for food.

They often do this in the summer, when it is light all day and all night.

Reindeer rest more during the night or just after feeding.

Sometimes they lie down to sleep, but they can also sleep standing up.

W t r y reindeer like?

baby

Mother reindeer give birth to a single baby once a year.

Babies are often born in the morning and start travelling with the herd within hours.

A baby reindeer is called a calf.

After about three or four months the calf grows **antlers** and learns to survive without its mother.

antlers

fur

nose

hooves

active busy doing lots of things

antlers hard body parts that grow on a reindeer's head

Arctic area surrounding the North Pole. It is very cold in the Arctic.

lichen plants that look like moss and that have no leaves, stem, or roots

mammal animal that feeds its babies milk. All mammals have some hair or fur on their bodies.

wolverines strong weasels known for their fierce hunting skills

Fin... ...t m...r

Websites

kids.nationalgeographic.com/kids/animals/creaturefeature/caribou/

In some places reindeer are also called caribou. Watch a video and find out more about them on this website.

www.biokids.umich.edu/critters/Rangifer_tarandus/

Find out all about reindeer on this BioKids website.

Index

Arctic 8, 9
antlers 5, 15, 21, 22
enemies 14, 15
feeding 6, 10, 11, 12, 13, 18
fur 6, 7, 22
groups 16, 17, 20

hooves 6, 13, 22
mammal 4
nose 7, 22
rest 19
size 4
swimming 11
young 4, 14, 20, 21